PROFES

SKILL

A guide to help buyers and sellers of writing services
get on the same page with quality and price.

Byron White | Founder WriterAccess

All inquires should be addressed to:

WriterAccess
240 Commercial Street
Suite 3B
Boston, MA 02109

http://www.idealaunch.com
http://www.writeraccess.com

International Standard Book Number: 978-1-60275-058-6

This book is intended for use as an informational guide and entertainment purposes and should not be used as a substitute for any professional medical care or treatment, professional legal advice or professional financial guidance.

TABLE OF CONTENTS

Foreword

By Casey Joseph
Casey Joseph Marketing

As a content strategist and copywriter, I have been on both sides of the conversation about quality and pricing.

As a buyer, I understand the nebulousness that can characterize the dialogue on this topic between businesses and writers. I also recognize that the market is laden with writing services misrepresenting quality or just not tackling its definition. It was in pursuit of clarity in this area that I was pleased to come across WriterAccess and Byron White.

As a writer, knowing my expectations frees me to create within those expectations -- similar to a dancer understanding the parameters of the studio space or a jazz soloist knowing the chord progressions of song. Having this freedom to create is essential to my ability to produce high-quality writing.

In this book, steered by his expertise as a content marketer, speaker, writer and entrepreneur, Byron has delved deeply into the complex topic of writing and emerged with a simple, useful convention; a convention that offers buyers and writers a means to match their expectations about quality and pricing, and improve their communication.

Infused with Byron's insights and charisma, this guide promises to be a boon to both authors and purchasers of content.

Note from Byron

You need quality content to engage readers orbiting at high speeds these days. But gathering ideas, developing stories and publishing the steady stream of quality content everyone needs to be successful take a lot of work and time.

For the last 15 years, I've been focused on helping thousands of customers create and optimize tens of millions of words and hundreds of thousands of content assets. At WriterAccess, we screen thousands of writers and match them daily with thousands of clients using new-age algorithms and performance technology.

What is most clear to me is this: the secret to content marketing is great writing from great writers. If you hire great writers, you will grow your marketing and sales at an accelerated rate. If you hire lousy writers, you will remain stagnant with content that simply does not connect with readers or search engines, and be forced to feed the pipeline of sales with traditional marketing that will eventually become extinct.

The challenge of this book is to provide a guide for both buyers and sellers of writing services on what to expect when you pay more. By breaking down the elements of quality writing with specific samples, we hope to get both writers and buyers on the same page.

INTRODUCTION

Quality writing is the new way, and frankly the only way, to engage readers and keep them coming back for more. With attention spans somewhere near zilch and online reading choices somewhere near a bazillion, you need quality prose to snag the attention of readers orbiting at high speeds.

You can go about getting that quality writing one of two ways. You can blindly throw a dart into the wind and hope to hit your target. Or you can go with an online marketplace that continuously rates and scores writers, letting you choose the level of expertise your projects demand.

The secret is to know what quality you should expect for the price you pay. That's what this guide is all about. We hope it enlightens, entertains and keeps you reading – while imbuing the value of quality content.

How This Guide Works

Just like you can't buy a Cadillac at Chevy prices, you're not going to get the highest quality writing for the lowest price. Writers with the skills and experience to produce high-caliber work deserve fair pay and wages that increase to match the level of quality.

To better illustrate exactly what you get when you pay more, we decided to showcase various samples, exemplifying different levels of skill and proficiency. Hopefully, the samples give you the gist of what we mean when we say you get more when you pay more.

The Assignment for the Samples

All the samples created by our designated writer heed this request: **Explain how the WriterAccess Star Rating system works.** We limited the writer to 150 to 250 words and asked for a system overview, not a step-by-step approach.

Our hope is the writer's samples demonstrate advancement of writing skills with each progression, providing insight on what you might expect when you pay for a Cadillac versus a Chevy. And please note that we're not using foreign automobiles in our analogy – we're currently representing only US-based writers!

The Star Rating System

Each writer that joins WriterAccess receives a star rating of 2 to 6 based on a manual review of his or her work and a stringent writing proficiency test. But establishing an initial star rating is just the beginning. An algorithm then keeps track of each writer's ongoing performance, tracking things like approval ratings, customer reviews, Love List statuses and successful order deliveries, automatically adjusting star ratings on the fly. Writers' star ratings fluctuate with performance.

We're constantly fine-tuning and improving our scoring technology and star rating methodology. Customers with low to mid-level budgets can find generalist writers to quickly crank out basic work. Customers with higher budgets and more complex requirements can access certified copywriters, tech writers, and/or journalists for the higher quality they demand for their investment. It's a winning proposition for both customers and writers.

Writers' Pay Rates

As mentioned, we rate all writers on a scale of 2 to 6. Writers with 2 to 5 stars earn between 2 cents and 8 cents per word for assignments that can be researched and turned around fairly rapidly. The price per word nets about $10 to $20 per hour for research writers. Six star writers are a cut above, earning 10 cents to $1 dollar per word depending on the skill requirements and the project visibility and complexity. Six star writers undergo special testing so we can verify their special skills, then receive a performance score for copywriting, technical writing and/or journalism. All 6 star writers are proven professionals with track records a mile long, earning (and deserving!) an estimated $25 to $100 per hour for their time.

Six Star Writing Pricing Variables

Complexity

Low (10 Cents/Word)

Experiential Writing

Thought Execution

Product Descriptions

Common Speak

Push Marketing

Storytelling

Execution

Samples that Guide

High ($1/Word)

Research Required

Thought Leadership

Product Motivation

Complex Lingo

Inbound Marketing

Story Magic

Ideation

Innovation Required

Visibility

Low (10 Cents/Word)

Product/Service Page

<1,000 Readers/Month

<1,000 Subscribers

Reader Low Proficiency

High ($1/Word)

Brand/Home Page

>10,000+ Readers/Day

>50,000+ Subscribers

Reader High Proficiency

Skills

Low (10 Cents/Word)

Logic

Articulation

Voice Execution

Voice Creation

Visibility/Clarity

Creativity

High ($1/Word)

Word Choice

Transitions

Professionalism

Analogies

Cohesiveness

Publishing Readiness

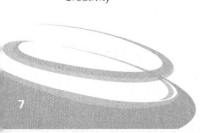

Sample Assessments

Do keep in mind that all writing in general runs the gamut from Plain Jane (or Joe) to copy that sizzles. Our goal with this guide is to explain the variation with assessments. The samples progress from the first to the last, so be sure to start with the first. Our skill and price assessment with each sample aims to represent the characteristics you might expect when you pay more.

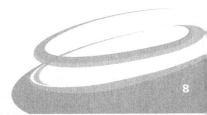

2 TO 6 STAR
RESEARCH WRITING

Research writers are skilled at diving into any assignment and surfacing with great work that meets the customers' requirements. The challenge becomes gauging how deep the writer needs to dive and the extent of time it will take to polish the work and make it shine. You meet that challenge when you start looking for writers in the 2 to 6 star research writing zone.

Standard Assessments

As pointed out in our assessments following each sample you're about to read, all of our research writers are going to deliver work with the basic requirements. Even 2 star work comes with accurate grammar, spelling and punctuation, as writers can't get through our entrance gates without it!

Our assessment of the 3 star work notes the increase in skill you pay for, evidenced by a variation of sentence structure and overall improved flow. Dive a writer deeper at the 4 star level and you'll discover enhanced organization, increased complexity and more precise word choices.

Engage a writer at the 5 star level and you're paying for the experience that delivers prose perked up with creativity. And, as our assessment notes, diving with our 6 star crew takes you to the sweetest depths of stellar research writing, producing a piece polished up with an added layer of finesse.

Please note that the 6 star writers you get at the research writing level may additionally be certified in one of our specialties, or they may not. Either way, the top earning tier of our research writing is 10 cents per word. Our 6 star crew earns it, consistently delivering the pearls that keep readers coming back for more.

SAMPLE 1

2 STAR RESEARCH WRITING @ 2 CENTS PER WORD

WriterAccess has a Star Rating system for its writers. It rates the quality of work each writer produces on a scale of 2 to 6. The writers get a star rating when they first join WriterAccess. Their rating can change as they produce work that is good or bad. Good work gets rated on the high end of the scale with a 5 or 6.

They must have quality writing to enter the system at all. Writers will be rejected unless they pass a test and editorial reviews of their resume, profile and writing samples. An algorithm keeps track of how good or bad the work is as they keep on writing. The writers' ratings can change based on things like how fast they finish assignments, customer reviews of their work and how many revisions they usually have to do.

Writers can move up the scale with good work. You can pick what star rating you want your orders to have and, as they say, "You get what you pay for."

SAMPLE 1 ASSESSMENT

2 STAR RESEARCH WRITING @ 2 CENTS PER WORD

Skills and Proficiency

Since our writers must jump through hoops to even enter our system, you can be sure that even 2 star work will have proper grammar and correct spelling. You're also sure to get the subject-verb agreements, proper verb conjugations and all other basic skills writers have ingrained in their brains from Writing 101.

But 2 star work won't have much else. You'll note the highly simplistic sentence structure, the use of cliché, the repetition of words and unsophisticated word choices. For instance, this writer uses phrases like "good or bad" instead of "high-quality and of lesser caliber."

Just because the writing may be simple, however, doesn't mean it won't meet the simplest needs. This level of writing may be ideal for the short and sweet blog entry or a quick product description that doesn't require festooning.

You may also be pleasantly surprised by much of the 2 star work, as these writers are aiming to climb up the scale to higher ranks. And the way to do that at WriterAccess is to consistently deliver writing that shines.

Pricing

• Accurate spelling, grammar and punctuation – 2 cents

Total = 2 cents per word

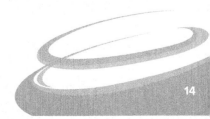

SAMPLE 2

3 STAR RESEARCH WRITING @ 4 CENTS PER WORD

Clients can choose the level of writing that fits their budget due to the Star Rating system at WriterAccess. Every writer gets a star rating that can go up or down based on the ongoing quality of their work. For research writing orders, 2 stars is the lowest rating and 6 stars is the highest. If a writer really shines, they can get even higher ratings and become eligible to work on even more advanced orders or assignments.

An algorithm keeps track of each writer's ongoing work. It reviews different factors, such as order completion time, customer reviews, frequency of revisions and other things. All writers must be good enough to rate at least 2 stars to become a writer with WriterAccess. WriterAccess makes every writer go through a difficult "entrance exam," followed by a stringent editorial review of writing samples, profile and resume.

Once writers are part of the WriterAccess "club," they can move up the scale and keep earning stars as long as they keep on producing quality work.

SAMPLE 2 ASSESSMENT

3 STAR RESEARCH WRITING @ 4 CENTS PER WORD

Skills and Proficiency

This 3 star writer exhibits the research writing skill set needed to deliver acceptable work while incorporating a variation in sentence structure that improves the writing's overall flow. You may still find less-than-ideal word choices, which this writer apparently tried to get around by using quotes around "entrance exam" and "club."

You're up a notch from the 2 star work, but you'll still find word choice remains a bit unsophisticated (i.e. "up or down"), as does the overall vibe. This is not the level of writing you'd want to showcase on your homepage, but it may be ideal for blog posts, quick articles or a series of brief product or service explanations.

On the plus side of the 3 star work, the final product is definitely readable and free of errors. You can also tell the writer understands the topic and is able to lay it out in a way that is informative and easy for the reader to comprehend.

As with the 2 star research writers, our 3 star batch of scribes are eager to climb up the scale and may wow you with results that can certainly help them get there.

Pricing

• Accurate spelling, grammar and punctuation – 2 cents

• Sentence structure variation and improved flow – 2 cents

Total = 4 cents per word

SAMPLE 3

4 STAR RESEARCH WRITING @ 6 CENTS PER WORD

When you need quality work, you know you can turn to WriterAccess, an online marketplace that uses a Star Rating system to let you select the specific level of quality of the work you need. Writers at the 2 star level will deliver the basics, while those writing at the 5 or 6 star levels will deliver higher-caliber work.

Writers are first introduced to the star rating system when they enter the system, provided they pass the writing proficiency test and a stringent editorial review of their resume, profile and writing samples. Their initial star rating can increase or decrease based on the quality of work they continue to deliver, with the quality gauged by a complex algorithm.

The algorithm looks at order completion times, client feedback, reviews and revision requests to track each writer's work on an ongoing basis. A writer who continues to shine can continue to climb up the rating scale ladder, while clients can continue to pick and choose the quality level of work that matches the specific order at hand.

SAMPLE 3 ASSESSMENT

4 STAR RESEARCH WRITING @ 6 CENTS PER WORD

Skills and Proficiency

This 4 star writer is confident about her writing. She is not afraid to start the piece with an attention-grabber that draws readers in, nor is she hesitant about throwing in a bit of rhyme with the phrase "continue to shine can continue to climb."

The work is well-organized and flows gracefully, devoid of choppy and mundane sentence structure. Intelligent word choice and a polished feel add a layer of professionalism to the piece.

Four star research writing lands you firmly in the middle of the pack, with writers who have enough experience to merit a solid ranking and the talent that serves to keep them there. This level can be ideal for blog posts or articles that require a bit more research than the lower-level orders. It can also be a good fit with a series of simple product descriptions or blurbs you may need around your website.

Four star writers have proved their worth, but many are not done yet. They, too, aim to scale up the ladder to higher ratings and may certainly do so by producing work that exceeds expectations.

Pricing

• Accurate spelling, grammar and punctuation – 2 cents

• Sentence structure variation and improved flow – 2 cents

• Organization, complexity and word choice – 2 cents

Total = 6 cents per word

SAMPLE 4

5 STAR RESEARCH WRITING @ 8 CENTS PER WORD

Let the stars guide you to the quality writing you need when you opt for a writer from WriterAccess. The online market place employs a dynamic Star Rating system that ranges from 2 to 6 stars for research writing orders, allowing you match your budget and requirements with the quality of writing you receive.

Go for the lowest level, 2 star writing, if you have a stingy budget and need only the bare bones of proper grammar and spelling. Hit higher in the heavens with 6 star writing if you need work that brilliantly shines.

Each writer is assigned a star rating upon entering the system, which is no easy feat to begin with. Writers must pass a tough proficiency test as well as an editorial review of their writing samples, profile and resume. Such factors play a role in their initial rating, but the rating system doesn't stop there.

A continuously updated algorithm keeps track of each writer's ongoing performance, adjusting the star rating as necessary. Ratings can increase or decrease based on factors that include delivery times, client reviews and revision requests.

The star rating system not only gives writers incentive to maintain high performance levels, but it ensures clients receive the quality writing they need and come to expect from WriterAccess.

SAMPLE 4 ASSESSMENT

5 STAR RESEARCH WRITING @ 8 CENTS PER WORD

Skills and Proficiency

Five star writers have been around the block quite a few times and their writing definitely shows it. Their talent and experience are evident, with complex sentence structures that keep readers engaged yet still remain straightforward enough to easily comprehend.

Their organizational skills are generally high, with a logical flow that keeps things streamlined. Careful word choices are another strong suit of the 5 star research writers, and they are likely to be good pals with a quality dictionary and thesaurus.

Creativity comes into the mix for this writer with the use of the star theme, while the use of examples provides readers with a better understanding of the topic at hand. The piece opens by piquing reader curiosity and closes neatly with a skilled wrap-up.

Move into 5 star territory and you're moving into writing that could perk up your website, grab attention through your articles and make your product descriptions sizzle.

Pricing

• Accurate spelling, grammar and punctuation – 2 cents

• Sentence structure variation and improved flow –2 cents

• Organization, complexity, clarity and word choice – 2 cents

• Creativity and engagement – 2 cents

Total = 8 cents per word

SAMPLE 5

6 STAR WRITING @ 10 CENTS PER WORD

When it comes to finding the ideal writer for a specific project, you can leave guessing games to the genies if you go with WriterAccess. This online marketplace uses a fine-tuned Star Rating system to make the perfect writer-client match. You simply pick your desired level that aligns with your desired results.

Star ratings range from 2 to 6 for research writing, with 6 star writers having the opportunity to advance to certified status for copywriting, tech writing and journalism. An initial star rating is assigned once writers get in the door, a feat only complete after passing a proficiency exam and manual review of their writing samples, profile and resume.

A computerized algorithm takes over from there, adjusting each writer's star rating after the completion of each assignment. Stars can rise with positive customer reviews and endorsements, Love List inclusions and other positive factors. Likewise, stars can fall with late deliveries, shoddy feedback and orders that fail to meet expectations.

Pick from level 2 to 6 for your research writing, going even higher for more exclusive projects that deserve the touch of a certified copywriter, tech writer or journalist. You'll never have to guess at what to expect, nor will you be wondering if the writer you choose is up for the task. If a guessing-game genie could do all that, there's a good bet he wouldn't keep getting shoved back in a bottle.

SAMPLE 5 ASSESSMENT

6 STAR WRITING @ 10 CENTS PER WORD

Skills and Proficiency

Welcome to the world of Cadillac, with 6 star writing that is at the top of the research writing order rank for a reason. The writing boasts all the impressive qualities of our 5 star writers along with one final polish of finesse that earns the full 10 cents per word.

The finesse in this case comes from the delightful references to a guessing-game genie. The reference pops up at the beginning and end of the piece, bringing full closure and leaving readers on a positive, playful note.

More finesse is evidenced by the attention-grabbing opening, the careful word choice and fluid transitions. The writing flows naturally. This writer was also able to include copious details without careening readers off on tangents or leaving them scratching their heads.

Readers feel content in their knowledge of the Star Rating system after reading this piece. They are also left with a feel-good vibe, and maybe even a chuckle, with the image of a genie being crammed back in a bottle.

Pricing

• Accurate spelling, grammar and punctuation – 2 cents

• Sentence structure variation and improved flow –2 cents

• Organization, complexity, clarity and word choice – 2 cents

• Creativity and engagement – 2 cents

• Top coat of finesse – 2 cent

Total = 10 cents per word

NOTE TO RESEARCH WRITERS

Just so you know, we think all of you are stars, even if you are not at the 6 star level. Achieving 6 stars may take some work and practice on your part, but it is certainly a possibility.

Here come a few quick tips on what's expected at the different Star Ratings for our Professional Writers

2 Star: You passed the entrance requirements and show promise. You're able to clearly present key information, an organized structure and avoid obvious (and embarrassing) spelling or grammatical errors.

3 Star: You enjoyed a solid score on your proficiency exam and have at least a bit of writing experience under your belt. Your writing meets the level 2 standards and additionally displays structural variation to retain reader interest. You may benefit from being more careful with word choices and striving to find the right word(s) to suit the context and get your point across.

4 Star: You scored pretty darn well on the proficiency test and have engaging writing samples to back up your level of experience. Your confidence comes across with strong word choices, keen organizational skills and ability to make the writing flow. Your star may increase a notch with repeated practice and additional experience that can make your work even more polished than it already is.

5 Star: Climbing to the 5 star ranks takes experience, proficiency and a super-strong portfolio. You enjoy the ability to match your tone, style and word choice to best suit a variety of assignment types without losing the clear and concise nature of your work. Your creativity comes through with playful word choices (when appropriate) while your mastery of language consistently produces a compelling and informative read.

6 Star: This master level of research writing orders is yours due to a consistently creative production of awesome work. You may have topped off at the level 5 for a spell, but sensational customer reviews and endorsements, timely deliveries, exceeding expectations and other positive influencers propelled you to the top.

6 STAR
COPYWRITING

Let's face it: great copywriting has snap, crackle and pop that stops readers in their tracks. It turns browsers into believers, and believers into buyers. It's also where our 6 star Certified Copywriting comes in, with a price range from 10 cents to $1 per word.

Customers need big-time quality and they can expect just that when they place 6 star orders. Our 6 star copywriters deliver the professional content sought for projects that demand high visibility, ideation, research and skill requirements.

6 Star Copywriting Assessments

Our assessments following the copywriting samples point out the steady increase in professionalism you enjoy with our 6 star certified copywriters. The baseline projects that earn 10 cents per word merit the pay with work that is logical, articulate and super-ready for publication.

As you climb up the price point scale, you'll note an increase in skills. Pay 25 cents per word and you're graced with smooth transitions, precise word choice and analogies. Up your rate to 50 cents per word and you get crisp and clean organization and professionalism.

Mastery kicks in at the 75 cents per word rate, as do elegance, confidence and revisions so skilled you'd never guess the writer may have spent considerable time producing them. Top off your copywriting at the $1 per word rate and you're getting the proverbial cherry on top. Extensive research, heightened proficiency, high visibility and even higher creativity seal the deal at our highest certified copywriting rate.

SAMPLE 6

6 STAR COPYWRITING @ 10 CENTS PER WORD

WriterAccess prides itself on its industry-leading Star Rating system, which is meant to match client demands with writer ability and skills.

Writers don't even enter the system unless they pass a difficult proficiency test and survive an editorial review of their writing samples, profile and resume. Once in, the rating process continues with a stringent review of each writer's ongoing performance.

An algorithm based on factors such as completion times, customer reviews, bonus pay and revision requests feed into the equation, constantly keeping track of where every writer stands. Writers are encouraged to work their way up the star rating ladder and are given the tools to do so with client and editorial feedback, an on-the-spot help desk and the forever-vigilant computerized system that keeps an eagle eye on their progress.

Clients receive a clear picture of what they can expect based on the level writer they choose, resulting in an end product that meets their needs and serves up a superior ROI.

SAMPLE 6 ASSESSMENT

6 STAR COPYWRITING @ 10 CENTS PER WORD

Skills and Proficiency

Even the most basic 6 star copywriting is good stuff. This writer delivers a piece that is polished and professional, suitable for a number of different projects that deserve streamlined copy.

The writing is straightforward and logical, offering an explanation that is easy and painless for the reader to follow and comprehend. The use of specialized terminology, such as "ROI," adds a level of professionalism while proving the writer is well-versed in the topic.

The 10 cent word rate offers a dash of spice with clever word choices and a carefully crafted structure, making it an ideal fit for website copy, newsletters and advanced product descriptions that merit more attention than the lower levels of research writing.

What the 10 cent per word piece lacks, however, is the full snap, crackle and pop treatment you find at the higher rates. While it makes a good read indeed, it has only dashes of spice rather than the full pump of pizzazz.

Pricing

• Logic – 3 cents

• Articulation – 3 cents

• Publication readiness – 4 cents

Total = 10 cents per word

SAMPLE 7

6 STAR COPYRIGHTING @ 25 CENTS PER WORD

Every writer is a star at WriterAccess, thanks to the agency's Star Rating system. Clients can pick how bright a star they need based on the demands of their individual assignments, although all assignments are completed by writers who put a lot of work into earning those stars.

To be accepted by WriterAccess, writers must pass a rigorous online test that assesses their grammar, spelling, organizational abilities and other technical skills. They are then subjected to an editorial review of their writing samples, profile and resume, receiving feedback from our editors when warranted.

Only then are writers accepted into the system, but the due process doesn't stop there. Writers are given an initial star rating which can increase (or decrease) depending on their performance going forward. WriterAccess developed an algorithm that combines various factors, such as client reviews, delivery times and bonus pay, which can boost or diminish the writer's overall rating.

Clients that opt for the top-notch certified writers can expect the most brilliant of results. The higher the rate, the more brilliant the results — it's up to you on how dazzling you need your universe to be.

SAMPLE 7 ASSESSMENT

6 STAR COPYRIGHTING @ 25 CENTS PER WORD

Skills and Proficiency

The prose enjoys the added snap that comes with the certified copywriting rate of 25 cents per word. This writer chose an overall theme with which to pepper the work, consistently drawing on a mention of stars to add a bit of zip to the finished product.

Analogies are common in writing at this rate, as are super-smooth transitions that help the work flow effortlessly. Deliberate word choices are another hallmark of our certified copywriters, and they are frequently not afraid to add a playful punch when merited.

Work at this rate is ideal for higher-end product descriptions, blogs, newsletters, articles and mid-level web copy. The piece is fun to read, thanks to the creative twists and clever turns.

There is no doubt the writer paid acute attention to her work, and it shows. The writing is professional yet features a friendly tone that makes a reader feel comfortable and informed.

Pricing

• All qualities of 10 cents per word copy PLUS:

 • Transitions – 5 cents

• Analogies – 5 cents

• Word choice – 5 cents

Total = 25 cents per word

SAMPLE 8

6 STAR COPYRIGHTING @ 50 CENTS PER WORD

Hate negotiations and haggling? Sick of hoping sheer luck will land you the perfect writer for your content? The online writing agency WriterAccess eliminates those concerns with its Star Rating system.

The system utilizes a specialized formula for summarizing the skill level of different writers, which helps clients pick the best writers for their needs. It also puts the payment rates on a logical basis without requiring extensive negotiations each time.

The writers are carefully screened in a multi-stage process that involves computerized testing and editorial screenings. Writers who pass are assigned an initial star rating while an algorithm keeps track of performance and refines each writer's star rating over time.

 The process streamlines the logistical overhead for both clients and writers, makes the payment rates seem more logical, and helps both the customers and the writers focus on the content itself, which after all is what really matters.

SAMPLE 8 ASSESSMENT

6 STAR COPYRIGHTING @ 50 CENTS PER WORD

Skills and Proficiency

This work crackles keenly with professionalism, featuring a crisp, clean delivery that merits the full 50 cents per word. While the piece is highly organized, the organizational structure is nearly transparent, a skill that comes with extensive experience and plenty of practice.

A logical flow is a given at this rate, as are the varying sentence structures and word choices that retain reader interest. A compelling intro serves to draw readers in, while the piece ties up neatly in the end.

The 50 cent per word rate produces copy that most would be proud to display on their website, provided they are not after the full carnival of words that come with the next levels. The copy here is solid, no-nonsense and confident, perfect for work that requires clarity but not necessarily a full acrobatic performance.

The writer has done her homework, figured out a logical organization for the material, and expressed all the key points clearly and without awkward or clunky distractions. Layer on the amazing flow and the writer has clearly earned 50 cents per word. Boost the copywriting rate and you're rewarded with writing that crackles.

Pricing

• All qualities of 25 cent per word copy PLUS:

• Professionalism – 10 cents

• Organization – 15 cents

Total = 50 cents per word

SAMPLE 9

6 STAR COPYWRITING @ 75 CENTS PER WORD

Identifying the best writer for a freelance assignment, as well as a fair payment rate, can be a tough call. It can be especially tough when you rely on fate, luck or accident for your desired results. WriterAccess instead relies on science using an industry-leading Star Rating system designed to deliver content with that snap, crackle and pop you demand.

We start with the world's finest proprietary writing tests, followed by careful portfolio reviews by seasoned professional editors. If the writer makes it past the initial hurdles and starts serving our clients, we continue to closely track a vast range of metrics. Customer reviews, revision request rates, time to delivery, bonus tip payments and more go into each writer's rating equation. Using algorithms fine-tuned over years of experience, we translate all this data into a unified star ratings system that match clients, assignments and writers at the fairest possible rate.

The result? Content marketers who achieve their objectives and writers who advance their careers — a win-win for everyone.

SAMPLE 9 ASSESSMENT

6 STAR COPYWRITING @ 75 CENTS PER WORD

Skills and Proficiency

Pop! goes the writer's skill and proficiency. No matter how much work this piece took, the end result is prose that seems inevitable, almost effortless. The final sentence is technically ungrammatical, but the writer has the assurance to pull this off — it's obviously not an accident.

The sentences enjoy an elegant internal flow, and they relate to the adjacent sentences and to the passage as a whole in a logical fashion that leaves the reader feeling informed and satisfied. The use of the first-person plural subject, "we," further draws the reader in, as they are being informed by a knowledgeable friend rather than just words on the page.

Here you get a writer with true mastery of the language both at the sentence level and in terms of overall logic, rhythm, and flow. The piece is easily suitable for a higher-end article, newsletter or website, or even blogs discussing a more complex topic.

The writing is steeped with confidence and is not ashamed to shine. These writers do their homework, sweat the details and carefully revise their prose before submitting it, earning that 75 cents.

Pricing

• All qualities of 50 cent per word copy PLUS:

• Mastery – 10 cents

• Revisions – 3 cents

• Confidence – 2 cents

• Elegance – 10 cents

Total = 75 cents per word

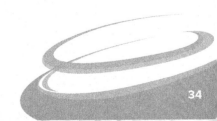

SAMPLE 10: PREMIUM COPYWRITING

6 STAR COPYRIGHTING @ $1 PER WORD

Observing a fine writer stumble through a project they're unsuited for can be painful — something like watching a confused gazelle trying to imitate an eagle. Animal antics can be hilarious at times, but you don't want that kind of mismatch in your project. That's why the WriterAccess Star Rating system doesn't just test for technical proficiency (although it certainly does that) — it aims for the soul as well as the gears of writing.

Well, we may be mixing up zoology, religion, and mechanics a bit too much here, but the point is clear enough: pairing up the right writers and assignments is both a science and an art. WriterAccess's star ratings rely on the world's best computerized proficiency tests, a team of professional editors to conduct portfolio reviews, and a wide range of ongoing metrics based on customer feedback, revision request rates, delivery time, bonus tip payments, and more. But sophisticated algorithms are useful only when the process is overseen by experts with years of experience; that's when you get truly great matches between clients, projects, and writers.

Hey, look — there's that gazelle again — only now it's doing what it does best: running like a dream. We're also doing what we do best: helping content marketers meet their goals, and writers advance their careers. So we can all soar like eagles.

SAMPLE 10 ASSESSMENT

6 STAR COPYRIGHTING @ $1 PER WORD

Skills and Proficiency

This work balances seemingly effortless prose, colorful imagery (of animals), and a carefully worked out overall structure. The combo entertains enough to retain the reader while conveying the essential technical or sales information in a way that's palatable and even memorable. Yes, you've finally met the full snap, crackle and pop!

The structure is a careful balance, rather than a sprinkling of colorful imagery at random. The middle paragraph contains the informational core, sandwiched between two entertainment-oriented paragraphs. The conclusion circles back to the intro to create a sense of closure.

The opening image of the gazelle is (purposely) slightly unpleasant to build tension, but the happy ending resolves this, while tying in nicely to the sales point. Thesaurus use is in full throttle, with synonyms or word repetition engaged as needed to establish the parallel in the (slightly far-fetched) analogy being crafted.

The writer has done his homework, demonstrated command of the topic, flushed out the piece with personality, and earned the full $1 per word. You get the full snap, crackle, pop of creative writing, with the perfect touch of mild humor that engages and entertains. And it's ready for prime-time, like a home page or better.

Pricing

• All qualities of 75 cent per word copy PLUS:

• Research – 4 cents

• Proficiency – 3 cents

• Visibility – 3 cents

• Creativity – 15 cents

Total = $1 per word

SPECIAL NOTE TO 6 STAR COPYWRITERS

We know you'd like to increase your own star rating to the 6 star copywriting level, and we'd like that, too. We're rooting for you! Check out a few quick tips on what's expected at the varying levels of our certified rankings.

10 Cents per Word: Necessary skills include clear organization, clear value proposition and the ability to make the writing flow seamlessly from one thought to the next. Varying sentence lengths help retain interest while descriptively hard-hitting word choices add a bit of spice without being too wordy or simplistic.

25 Cents per Word: Add a layer of creativity, finding a core theme that can tie all the ideas together. Make word choices careful, crafty and devoid of unnecessary padding or excess verbiage.

50 Cents per Word: Clear mastery of the topic at hand is required. Precision is a must, especially when it comes to choosing which details to include and which to omit. Skilled transitions add to the flow, as does a strong opening brought back home with a neat and tidy closing.

75 Cents per Word: Mastery of language here, using just the right word to express an idea or describe a concept, as if that word were created specifically for you to use at that exact moment. Your syntax flows, appearing effortless and inevitable. Your revisions and precision are skilled enough to make it appear as if the writing required little or no effort at all.

$1 per Word: Add another layer of pizzazz, now telling a story, expertly incorporating foreshadowing, conflict and then resolution as needed. Your writing needs to be as much fun to read as it is to create, with the power to persuade, entertain and make a lasting impact.

Depending on the assignment and its objective, this level may bring in a point of view, specific "voice" or personality and/or entertaining or captivating imagery. Careful! This should not feel awkward, forced or over-the-top. You need lots of practice to polish your prose to the 6 star copywriting level.

6 STAR
TECH WRITING

The goal of a high-quality technical writing is not to bowl you over with a bunch of tech mumbo jumbo that makes the reader feel like an idiot. In fact, the complete opposite is true. While the writer should be fully comfortable with and knowledgeable about the technical topic at hand, he or she should also be able to present it in a way that makes the reader feel comfortable, content and in-the-know.

6 Star Tech Writing Assessments

Similar to our 6 star copywriters, our certified tech writers must display an array of skills that move them into the high-tech zone. Our assessments of the tech writing samples outline how the skills increase as the pay increases, right along with your expectations.

Tech writing at 10 cents per word features the articulation and logic that gives it superb publication readiness, and the quality keeps rising from there. Invest in 25 cents per word and you can expect talented transitions, explanatory analogies and words chosen with precision.

Up the ante to 50 cents per word and you're boosting the attention to organization and professionalism. Mastery, confidence and a layer of elegance come with the 75 cents per word rate, as do careful revisions that produce smooth-as-silk results. Take it up one more notch to $1 per word for maximum-visibility tech writing that requires the highest level of research, proficiency and creativity.

SAMPLE 11

6 STAR TECH WRITING @ 10 CENTS PER WORD

While all marketplaces like WriterAccess depend on screening methodology and technology for success, WriterAccess takes the concept to an even higher level. The platform's proprietary algorithm and online tests remove the guesswork, delivering the quality of work clients pay for and expect when they place a writing order through the advanced system.

Writers only enter the system after successfully completing an online test and undergoing stringent manual reviews of their work samples and history. Their initial Star Rating is automatically adjusted as they continue to produce work in the system, based on the ongoing quality level of their work as determined by the algorithm.

Algorithms work around the clock, constantly calculating various factors and adjusting star ratings with every order completed. Factors include the number of revision requests, client ratings of the work, addition to or removal from client Love Lists and number of client endorsements.

Each writer's current star rating of 2 to 6 reflects the quality of their work to-date, providing clients with an accurate way to target exactly what they want and receive exactly what they need.

SAMPLE 11 ASSESSMENT

6 STAR TECH WRITING @ 10 CENTS PER WORD

Skills and Proficiency

You're definitely getting a professional piece at the 10 cents per word rate, along with a few other goodies that merit tech writer certification. The writing is clean, crisp and easy to understand, with an underlying confidence that makes it clear the writer knows her business.

A strong foundation serves as the backbone of the piece, sprinkled with just enough detail to provide full comprehension without distracting from the overall explanatory nature of the assignment. The readers are satisfied with the knowledge they just gleaned, thanks to the straightforward delivery.

With a strong, logical flow and precise articulation, this writing is publication ready. It's well-suited for a website, article or research project that requires a firm understanding of the topic to report back to readers in a way they can understand.

Ten cents per word gets you solidly sophisticated copy, but you'll still lack the full snap, crackle, pop you can expect at the higher rates of pay. Higher rates can come with details that are fleshed out a bit more and an added dose of flair.

Pricing

- Logic – 3 cents

- Articulation – 3 cents

- Publication readiness – 4 cents

Total = 10 cents per word

SAMPLE 12

6 STAR TECH WRITING @ 25 CENTS PER WORD

Technology is the secret weapon of WriterAccess, producing a continuously up-to-date Star Rating system that accurately matches clients and writers. The star rating system ranges from 2 to 6, and clients can target the quality level that accommodates their specific assignments and overall budget.

Clients may pick a 2 star writer for bulk orders or those that only require professional linguistic skills or opt for 6 star orders that deliver additional precision, expertise and creativity. The initial star rating of each writer is determined by his or her performance while meeting the entrance requirements. These include passing a proficiency exam and meeting standards determined during a manual review of writing samples, profile and resume.

Ongoing assessments of a writer's on-time deliveries, client rating of work, revision requests and endorsements and other algo influencers are continuously calculated by the ever-diligent algorithm, producing round-the-clock updates with the submission of each assignment.

Clients never need to wonder what level of work they should expect with each order. Writers are constantly performing at their optimum level to fuel the algorithm with positive influencers and clients with work that meets or exceeds expectations.

SAMPLE 12 ASSESSMENT

6 STAR TECH WRITING @ 25 CENTS PER WORD

Skills and Proficiency

This technical writer knows her stuff and presents it in a way readers can both understand and enjoy. You enjoy added snap at the 25 cents per word rate with writing that incorporates professional terminology without making the reader uncomfortable.

Though the writer had limited space, she does a good job of making room to provide an example to better illustrate her point. In this case, she chose to focus on why clients may want different quality levels, perhaps clearing up an unspoken question in readers' minds as to why anyone would opt for lower quality work at a lower rate.

Super-long sentence length is one of the caveats of detail-heavy writing, although this writer pulls it off. One fix for this piece might be to lose the repetition of stand-out words, such as influencer, as they initially pack a punch yet lose potency on the second run.

Nonetheless, the writing is logical, linguistically compelling and deserving of 25 cents per word. Work at this level work would be an asset for reports, websites and articles.

Pricing

• All qualities of 10 cents per word copy PLUS:

• Transitions – 5 cents

• Analogies – 5 cents

• Word choice – 5 cents

Total = 25 cents per word

SAMPLE 13

6 STAR TECH WRITING @ 50 CENTS PER WORD

WriterAccess combines top-level technology with precise screening methodology to consistently ensure writers deliver the quality work clients expect and deserve. The technological aspect consists of a continuously updated algorithm that weighs positive and negative influencers with the submission of every order. The screening methodology ensures only high-quality writers enter the system in the first place.

Successful entrance into the platform is only granted after writers pass a proficiency test and a manual review of their writing samples, profile and resume. They are then assigned an initial Star Rating from 2 to 6, which adjusts based on their ongoing performance levels as determined by the proprietary algorithm.

A 3 star writer, for example, may eventually move up in his ranks with work that is rich with positive influencers, such as Love List inclusions, ratings that exceed expectations and endorsements. He can likewise decrease in rank with a proliferation of negative factors, such as late delivery, below expectations ratings or an abundance of help desk tickets.

Writers, and clients, are able to ascertain the quality of work expected at any given moment, thanks to the constant calculations working diligently behind the scenes. The algorithm additionally contributes to the mass of data and intellectual property that becomes the nerve center for WriterAccess, and that nerve center fuels clients with the steady output of quality content that makes the platform and the clients a success.

SAMPLE 13 ASSESSMENT

6 STAR TECH WRITING @ 50 CENTS PER WORD

Skills and Proficiency

Pay 50 cents per word and you get a meticulous balance of technology and clear explanation that leaves readers fulfilled. They are satisfied that they truly understand what they just read and perhaps even a bit relieved that they were not subjected to unnecessary details.

Using phrases such as "behind the scenes" makes the work even more relatable. The average reader is typically more comfortable with language that veers toward common speak than they are with technical lingo, and this writer realizes and capitalizes on that concept.

The writer adds a crafty crackle to the work by outlining an example of a 3 star writer. While the example sticks with the facts, it reads more like a mini-story than a dry list of factual info.

Careful word choice, the nice nerve center analogy and streamlined organization sprinkle even more crackle on the finished product. This writing is well worth the 50 cents per word.

Pricing

• All qualities of 25 cent per word copy PLUS:

• Professionalism – 10 cents

• Organization – 15 cents

Total = 50 cents per word

SAMPLE 14

6 STAR TECH WRITING @ 75 CENTS PER WORD

WriterAccess combines high-end technology with a careful balance of human intervention to create a constantly updated Star Rating system for writers that catapults the platform into superstar status. The combination first kicks into gear while screening writers entering the system, with a computerized evaluation of their scores on an online proficiency test and a manual review of their resume, writing samples and profile.

An initial star rating is granted upon a writer's acceptance into the system, but writers must consistently meet high standards in order to maintain their current rating and achieve a higher rank. Star ratings range from 2 to 6 and a round-the-clock proprietary algorithm keeps track of a writer's performance with the submission of each assignment. Client reviews, ratings that meet, exceed or do not meet expectations, on-time deliveries and Love List inclusions or exclusions are calculated by the algorithm, updating the ratings accordingly.

Alas, just because something is high tech does not mean it is perfect. Manual overrides are often necessary, as machines don't always catch atypical nuances that can't be reflected in a systematic computerized analysis. Manual overrides may be required, for instance, if a customer doesn't specify requirements correctly and a writer delivers a product they only thought the client wanted. Overrides also ensure writers are not penalized for working below their star rating, such as a 6 star writer completing 3 star work if they so choose.

WriterAccess leverages the power of technology while providing a vital component for success: the human touch.

SAMPLE 14 ASSESSMENT

6 STAR TECH WRITING @ 75 CENTS PER WORD

Skills and Proficiency

Nice, no? Certified tech writing at the 75 cents per word rate usually is. Our writers at this rate are confident in their technological knowledge as well as their creativity, and they are not afraid to showcase both.

The word choices are careful, blending sophisticated terminology with colloquial language that makes the piece supremely easy to read. Additional pop! comes from the powerful delivery, making it evident the writer knows her stuff and has done her homework.

The diligent work and careful revisions it must have taken to produce a work of this caliber remain a mystery, as the writer makes them appear effortless. The beginning and end work together to bring home a very strong message: No matter how high-tech anything ever gets, it's the human touch that brings all things to life.

The characteristics in this piece all point to true writing mastery, and what you can expect at 75 cents per word.

Pricing

- All qualities of 50 cent per word copy PLUS:

- Mastery – 10 cents

- Revisions – 3 cents

- Confidence – 2 cents

- Elegance – 10 cents

Total = 75 cents per word

SAMPLE 15

6 STAR TECH WRITING @ $1 PER WORD

Writers that apply to WriterAccess better make fast friends with technology if they expect to succeed. That friendship begins by becoming familiar with phrases and concepts such as propriety algorithm, positive and negative algo influencers and a Star Rating system that mingles high-tech advances with human expertise. And it's not just the technical writers who should buddy-up with the techie stuff.

Technology plays a key role from the get-go, automatically eliminating writers that are unable to score satisfactorily on an initial proficiency test. The propriety algorithm takes over from there, with a customized equation created by the platform's founder that keeps tabs on various aspects of each writer's ongoing performance.

Writer Test

You correctly answered **15** of the **44** questions.

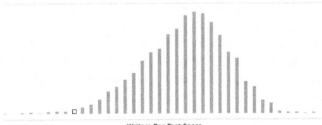

Writers Per Test Score

Writers enter the system with an initial star rating that automatically adjusts after each submission based on those negative or positive algo influencers. Negative influencers include late delivery and below expectation ratings while positive ones include client endorsements and Love List inclusions.

The human touch is also always present, starting with a manual review of writing samples, resumes and profiles at the onset and overriding algorithm calculations when factors crop up that the machine can't recognize. Substandard order instructions from clients that don't produce what clients wanted or writers working below their star ratings by choice are prime situations for overrides to ensure writers are not penalized. The carefully balanced combination keeps writers on-target, submissions top-notch and clients supremely satisfied since they'll always know what to expect.

SAMPLE 15 ASSESSMENT

6 STAR TECH WRITING @ $1 PER WORD

Skills and Proficiency

The crème de la crème of technical writing, the $1 per word rate gives you the delightful details that propel the writing from awesome to extraordinary. This writer provides visuals that can greatly enhance a reader's understanding of a technological topic while she also creates a storyline that draws in the reader and even evokes a bit of emotion.

Disbelief may erupt when readers learn even non-technical writers must make friends with technology, but the conflict is resolved throughout the piece and everyone lives "happily ever after" in the end.

Notice, too, how the writer explains concepts introduced in the intro in a classy and subtle manner, ensuring readers are never left feeling stupid for not knowing a definition or two.

If all that's not enough, a spark of humor polishes off this crème de la crème work, delivering a savory end product worth the rate. Pay $1 per word and you enjoy the full snap, crackle, pop of high-quality high-tech writing.

Pricing

- All qualities of 75 cent per word copy PLUS:

- Research — 4 cents

- Proficiency — 3 cents

- Cohesiveness — 3 cents

- Creativity — 15 cents

Total = $1 per word

SPECIAL NOTE TO
TECH WRITERS

Achieving Certified Tech writer status takes a big brain and mondo creativity, and we know many of you have both! If you're interested in applying for tech writer certification, check out a systematic series of tips on what you need to deliver for the varying levels and rates.

10 Cents per Word: Translating high-tech lingo into reader-friendly prose is a must for all levels of our Certified Tech writers. This level writing must also be devoid of spelling, grammatical and punctuation faux pas, boast an organized, logical flow and exhibit a keen understanding of the topic.

25 Cents per Word: Showing advanced knowledge of the subject matter is required here. Enhancing your work with targeted examples of what's being discussed helps, as does implementing a compelling introduction, conclusion and careful word choices.

50 Cents per Word: Here you're able to create a precise balance of high-tech and reader-friendly features, illustrated by your word choice, creative analogies and storytelling techniques.

75 Cents per Word: Creative techniques further enhance the writing at this level, and your obvious familiarity with the subject shines through.

$1 per Word: Acute reader awareness leaves the target audience feeling well-educated and satisfied with your spin, served up with aplomb. You effectively deploy an ongoing theme, point of view, specific "voice" or personality, storyline and/or other modes of creativity without detracting from the topic at hand.

High-tech caveat: Creative high-tech writers can never fake it. If you try faking the high-tech stuff, the writing is likely to come across as a jumble of muck that leads to more ques-tions than answers. Don't force the creative stuff. And stay away from the fluff.

6 STAR
JOURNALISM

Read a typical news story or blog post and (hopefully!) you get the gist of who, what, when, where, why and how. The 6 star journalists at WriterAccess know how to deliver the WOW. As with all our certified writers, our journalists are seasoned professionals who have paid their dues and earned their stars. Our journalists have the added skill of being able to tell a dang good story.

6 Star Journalism Assessments

Good storytelling is the cornerstone of all our 6 star journalism, with our assessments of the samples focusing on the various skills that come with each level. Even the most basic stories come with the logic, articulation and publication readiness that nets 10 cents per word.

Boost your journalism rate to 25 cents per word and you're pumping the story with sleek transitions, crafty analogies and careful word choice. Hit 50 cents per word and you can expect an additional layer of professionalism and keen organization that comes with the rate.

As our assessments will show, true mastery of storytelling is evident at the 75 cents per word rate. You'll also enjoy a piece brimming with confidence and elegance, thanks to streamlined revisions that make the work seem effortless. Take our journalism to the top level of pay at $1 per word and you can expect the top tier of creativity. Our top-notch journalism often involves deep research and is well-suited for high visibility pieces that really need to WOW.

SAMPLE 16

6 STAR JOURNALISM @ 10 CENTS PER WORD

WriterAccess founder Byron White might have a strong penchant for entrepreneurship, but he's not your typical serial entrepreneur. He doesn't hunker in the garage coming up with one fizzled idea after another while burning through the family savings and ticking off his wife.

He actually creates things that work.

One of the brilliant creations on his lengthy list of accomplishments is his exclusive Star Rating system for WriterAccess. The system, which rates writers from 2 stars to 6 stars, lets clients choose the quality level of writing they want to pay for and rewards to top-rated writers with the top-tier pay.

Top ratings are never an automatic given, but every writer has the freedom to earn them. Getting into the system is an accomplishment within itself, with writers required to pass a tough proficiency test and receive the nod from equally tough editors reviewing their writing samples, profile and resume. Each writer gets an initial star rating, which is continuously adjusted through White's winning algorithm.

The algorithm tracks order completion times, revision requests, customer reviews and bonus pay as it updates each writer's rank an ongoing basis. Clients never have to guess at the quality of work they should expect, while writers have ample encouragement to continue to produce great work.

The genius behind the system could only come from someone like White, whose past successes include more than 20 years as a freelance graphic artist rep, the establishment of platforms like WriterAccess and, yes, the continued support of his wife.

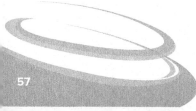

SAMPLE 16 ASSESSMENT

6 STAR JOURNALISM @ 10 CENTS PER WORD

Skills and Proficiency

Opt for one of our certified journalists and you're going to get a good story no matter what. This writer chose to bookend the piece with story tidbits, beginning and ending the work with info pertaining to WriterAccess founder Byron White.

And it's not just mundane info, either, as the writer includes a fun morsel meant to make readers chuckle. Such a detail also makes readers relate, as they are all likely to have had relationships where their partners offered undying support (or not).

The 10 cents per word rate gets you a smooth flow, a compelling lead that draws in the readers, and a closing that brings them full circle. The writing is professionally crafted, worthy of a corporate blog, article or similar outlet.

While this rate nets you work you can proudly display, the stories get even better from here. Beefier details coupled with the full snap, crackle, pop treatment are still down the line.

Pricing

- Logic – 3 cents

- Articulation – 3 cents

- Publication readiness – 4 cents

Total = 10 cents per word

SAMPLE 17

6 STAR JOURNALISM @ 25 CENTS PER WORD

You have robots that can vacuum your floor, toilets that flush by themselves and standardized tests that supposedly tell you if you happen to be a moron. But technology still hasn't found a way to accurately rate the tone, style and true excellence of a writer.

The Star Rating system and its algorithm at WriterAccess come close, though. Instead of relying wholly on mechanics, the system rates writers based on both technical and human-friendly variables. Delivery times, client feedback, bonus pay and revision requests enter the equation, all of which keep a keen eye on writers' ongoing performance and adjusts the star ratings accordingly. The rating system ranges from 2 stars to 6 stars, with pay rates that match the quality level.

Superior performance is expected from the get-go, with writers put through an inaugural round of human and technical reviews to even qualify for WriterAccess. Editors manually review profiles, resumes and writing samples while an online proficiency test tells a writer if, well, he or she happens to be a linguistic moron.

Writers hit the starting gate with an initial star rating, which automatically adjusts based on their ongoing performance. Clients pick and choose the quality level in which they want to invest while writers all have the chance to climb up the ladder of success. Top ratings come from more than analytics that don't take any human factors into consideration, just like you're not likely to find great writing clacking out of a robot.

SAMPLE 17 ASSESSMENT

6 STAR JOURNALISM @ 25 CENTS PER WORD

Skills and Proficiency

Pay the certified journalist rate of 25 cents per word and your story comes complete with a sizzling snap. As with our first journalism example, this piece again swiftly draws in readers, this time by making it personal.

The writer was able to pinpoint something to which all readers can relate: the advent of technology taking over their lives. The piece first sets the story by establishing the foundation of the ongoing theme of human vs. technology. It then delivers the facts without losing momentum or friendly tone.

Clever word choices help keep the theme going, with the ongoing juxtaposition of human vs. technology. The piece closes with one final swat at the robot, reinforcing how humans can do certain things better.

Corporate blogs would again benefit from this level of quality, which is as informative as it is fun to read. Heck, the fun factor alone merits the 25 cents per word, although you also get the snap outlined above.

Pricing

- All qualities of 10 cents per word copy PLUS:

- Transitions – 5 cents

- Analogies – 5 cents

- Word choice – 5 cents

Total = 25 cents per word

SAMPLE 18

6 STAR JOURNALISM @ 50 CENTS PER WORD

If dating websites used the WriterAccess system to create the perfect match, dating sites would soon go out of business. That's because WriterAccess developed a way to make a perfect match every time and, with so many perfect matches, they're would be no one left to date.

Thankfully, there are plenty of writers and clients looking for matches at WriterAccess, and they're matched up successfully through a no-fail Star Rating system. The system removes the guesswork by applying a fine-tuned balance of art and science to match writers with clients. Clients with lower budgets can opt for the 2 star end of the scale while those looking for high-end work can choose from the 6 star or certified writer pools.

An initial star rating is assigned to each writer upon entering the system, and the rating is adjusted after every order submission. An ever-vigilant algorithm calculates the scientific factors, such as client ratings, revision requests and on-time deliveries. Manual overrides kick into play when necessary to keep the artistic vibe going when science can't catch the nuances.

Art and science are also mingled during the writer qualification process. Computerized test scores from an online proficiency exam are combined with manual editorial reviews of writer profiles, writing samples and resumes.

The end result is a rating system that never leaves writers wondering where they stand or clients wondering about the quality of work they'll receive. Or, as noted, a perfect match every time.

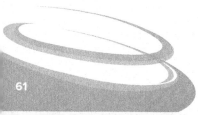

SAMPLE 18 ASSESSMENT

6 STAR JOURNALISM @ 50 CENTS PER WORD

Skills and Proficiency

Snap *and* crackle come at the 50 cents per word rate. The writer has obviously done her homework and knows the topic well. A clever comparison kicks off the piece, piquing reader interest from the get-go by stirring immediate curiosity about how online dating could go bankrupt.

The writer also targeted the so-called story behind the story by showcasing the magic balance of art and science that makes the system so effective. The work is professional, well-organized and sports a logical flow.

Certified journalists at the 50 cents per word rate have the experience and talent that produces a distinctly professional product. Their work boasts keen organization and a seamless flow.

Work of this caliber is easily suited for corporate blogs, feature articles, newspapers and magazines. Stories that snap and crackle are in high demand and well worth 50 cents per word.

Pricing

•All qualities of 25 cent per word copy PLUS:

• Professionalism – 10 cents

• Organization – 15 cents

Total = 50 cents per word

SAMPLE 19

6 STAR JOURNALISM @ 75 CENTS PER WORD

Finding the perfect writer can be a lot like fishing. You throw your lure out into the masses and hope to snag a compatible match. You have equal chances of catching a trout as you do hooking an old shoe, unless you go with the star rated writers at WriterAccess.

The Star Rating system at WriterAccess ensures you're making the perfect match every time, whether you're looking for a bulk can of tuna or a pricey salmon steak. That's because each writer is ranked according to the quality of his or her work on a continuous basis. Cast your line with the rate you're willing to pay, and one of the writers in the pool of professionals accepts your offer and delivers what you need.

Before writers can swim with the fishes, so to speak, WriterAccess screens out those that should get thrown back into the deep seas. Writers must pass a proficiency exam and be approved by big fish editors that review profiles, resumes and samples. An initial star rating comes with the initial launch into the platform, and writers can move up and down the scale based on their ongoing performance.

Writers with 2 stars can swim upstream to achieve the top-rated 6 stars, thanks to an algorithm that looks at customer reviews, delivery times, revision requests and other factors. WriterAccess makes sure you're never stuck with a can of worms when you could be deliciously dining on that salmon.

SAMPLE 19 ASSESSMENT

6 STAR JOURNALISM @ 75 CENTS PER WORD

Skills and Proficiency

Work that pops is what you get at the certified journalism rate of 75 cents per word. This is yet another fun piece of the type you may expect from our certified journalists, with a piece that is as easy to read as it is amusing.

This writer uses the ongoing theme of fishing as the bait to lure readers in, then sets up a conflict, continues the litany of effective analogies and closes the piece with a "delicious" ending.

Writing at this level can be highly effective for a creative press release, a super-creative newsletter entry, bulk emails that need to stand out from the crowd or feature articles covering just about anything.

Clever, captivating and full of creative twists is the norm for work at the 75 cent per word rate. You're a mere whisker away from the top of the line with work that would do any firm proud.

Pricing

• All qualities of 50 cent per word copy PLUS:

• Mastery – 10 cents

• Revisions – 3 cents

• Confidence – 2 cents

• Elegance – 10 cents

Total = 75 cents per word

SAMPLE 20

6 STAR JOURNALISM @ $1 PER WORD

Writers have to do much more than put pen to paper (or fingers to keyboard), especially when they're working under the Star Rating system of WritersAccess. They have to be sleuths, wordsmiths and repeat performers – all with an eagle-eyed overseer breathing down their necks. And the overseer isn't even human!

The sleuth part of the gig comes from hunting down facts, figures and other info needed to flesh out a story. Writers are typically given limited info on each client, topic, personality or possibilities that lie within.

The wordsmith factor kicks in before writers are even accepted into the WriterAccess platform. A brain-wracking proficiency test weeds out the folks who slept through English class while editors manually pore over resumes, samples and writer profiles. Once in, repeat performance is a must, thanks to the non-human overseer.

Call him Mr. Algorithm because he's the one in charge of adjusting a writer's star rating, which can range from 2 to 6. He looks at delivery times, customer reviews, bonus pay and revision requests to keep writers in top form.

The non-human nature of the beast means writers can't trick him. They can't sweet talk him. And they can't bribe him with candy bars or Jujubes. The only way to stay in his good graces is to keep on performing at the epitome of excellence.

SAMPLE 20 ASSESSMENT

6 STAR JOURNALISM @ $1 PER WORD

Skills and Proficiency

Certified journalism at the $1 per word rate delivers the full snap, crackle and pop that make the work truly remarkable. This piece additionally gives you the full gamut of characteristics that make a great story.

Your main characters are the protagonist writer and antagonist Mr. Algorithm, setting the stage for a classic conflict of man vs. machine. Readers can take sides to make the read more fun, although this journalist makes sure to provide balance by outlining both sides of the story.

Before you even get to the main conflict, you're served an enticing intro that makes you want to read more. The development of character unfolds throughout the piece, followed by the climax and its resolution nestled neatly at the conclusion.

Work of this caliber is ideal for a major publication with a real writer's byline crowning the top of it. It's also all yours for $1 per word.

Pricing

• All characteristics of 75 cents-per-word writing PLUS:

• Research – 4 cents

• Proficiency – 3 cents

• Cohesiveness – 3 cents

• Creativity – 15 cents

Total = $1 per word

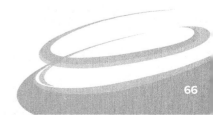

SPECIAL NOTE TO 6 STAR JOURNALISTS

We know many of you may feel you deserve 6 stars and journalism certification, and we want to help you get there. Please review a handful of tips on what's expected at the varying levels of our Certified Journalism rating system.

10 Cents per Word: Ability to tell a good story is a must for every rung on the Certified Journalism scale, as are clear organizational skills and writing that employs a smooth, logical flow. Drawing the reader in with a strong lead and escorting them out with a satisfying closing seal the deal for 10 cents per word.

25 Cents per Word: Layer on the ability to keep an ongoing story alive and you'll earn your 25 cents per word. Creativity, clever word choices and use of a groovy theme are added bonuses.

50 Cents per Word: Add even more pizzazz and you're hitting the 50 cents per word range. Strong and clever analogies, mastery of the topic, the establishment of a clear conflict, resolution and storyline help net this rate.

75 Cents per Word: Your mastery of the topic is enhanced by your mastery of storytelling. Your careful word choice, clever twists and turns, and seemingly effortless prose weaves a wonderful tale readers feel compelled to dive into and savor.

$1 per Word: You have the story all right, and then some. That "some" is your incredible skill, creativity and adroit way with words that shines through in every single sentence. Your piece is far beyond words on a page: it's a slice of life to which readers can relate as well as enjoy and learn from. Your ability to build tension is evident, as are your abilities to foreshadow, develop characters and bring it all home to a fulfilling close.

Now the warning: Those who are not innately gifted with the skills to do this can produce work that feels cheesy or contrived. This type of writing comes from the soul more than the brain, but it can also be developed in those that possess even a spark of it. Keep writing and developing your skills and you may be amazed at what you find inside.

BEFORE
AND AFTER
SAMPLES

Before and After Samples

Transforming content from good to great is challenging. To help make the transformation, we've put together lots of before and after samples that we hope inspire. You'll see samples from two companies, one that sells products, the other services. Be sure to download the guide and listen to a recording of Byron's presentation called Snap, Crackle and Pop Your Content to Engage and Convert. (See Resources)

 The before copy is typically boring, flat and likely to get passed by. It has little or no creativity, and misses the mark on most of the assessments in this guide.

 The after copy offers the "snap, crackle and pop" you need to engage readers and motivate action. It's at a much higher level, featuring the key elements of tone, style and creativity required for success.

Home Décor Company

About Us

 The Chic Casa Company was founded in 1983. The company makes blankets, tapestry hangings and other home décor. It makes a "Home Sweet Home."

 Chic Casa does more than make home décor. We create warmth, with a full line of cushy blankets, warm wall hangings and other sensational stuff to spruce up your living space. Since 1983 we've been turning houses, apartments and the starkest of offices into places you can call "Home Sweet Home."

Product Description

This red blanket is fleece, which is a good selling point. It is warm and cozy and makes the room brighter.

Warm your heart (and toes!) with this cozy red blanket. Brilliant scarlet hue adds pizzazz to any room while the fluffy fleece fends off the chilliest of temps.

Home Page

Welcome to the Chic Casa Company Home Page. Look around the website and you might find home décor you might like. You can buy things from the website or you can look in the retailer section that says where to buy it in stores.

You've just landed in a little bit of heaven, thanks to the warm and cuddly décor you'll find at Chic Casa. Our mission is to make every house feel like a cozy home, and we do so by offering you easy shopping right from our site as well as a list of local retailers where you can nab that bit of heaven right in your very own town.

Calls to Action

-- Click here to join the mailing list for the Chic Casa Company.

-- Click here to get a discount coupon for your first order.

-- Click here to get a FREE LAMP from the Chic Casa Company.

-- Want to be surrounded by warmth on a regular basis? Click here to join the Chic Casa mailing list.

-- Enjoy 10 percent off your first Chic Casa order by clicking here.

-- Enlighten your life with a free Chic Casa lamp.

Headlines

-- Read the Chic Casa Company Blog to See What is New and Exciting in Home Décor and Blankets and Other Things

-- The Chic Casa Company Has New Blankets for Fall and They Sold 5,000 of Them to a School District in Montana

-- House Need a Facelift? Check out What's New and Now in Chic Casa Home Décor

-- Find out Why 5,000 Montana Students Just Had to Have Chic Casa's New Fall Blankets

Welcome Emails

Thank you for signing up for the Chic Casa Company emails. The company will send you emails that have information on the latest home décor trends, news about home décor and exciting things that happen with the Chic Casa Company.

If you're not feeling completely hugged just yet, you will soon, once you start receiving your regular lineup of warm and cozy Chic Casa Company emails. Thanks for signing up!

We call our emails warm and cozy because they're always rich with info on the latest home décor trends, the greatest industry news and some pretty amazing company projects.

Announcement

The Chic Casa Company has a new offer and it involves giving you a FREE!!!!! home décor guide called "Making a House a Cozy Home." The thinking is that you will see things in the guide that the Chic Casa Company sells and then you will buy the things from the Chic Casa Company. The company is always honest so they are telling it "like it is."

Want to add a bit of warmth and charm to your home but not sure where to begin? Check out our "Making a House a Cozy Home" guide which serves up plenty of places to start. The Chic Casa home décor guide is free and furthers our overall mission of helping to transform every house into a "Home Sweet Home."

Email Header

-- Subject: Welcome New Chic Casa Company Customer

-- Subject: FREE!!!!! New Chic Casa Company Home Décor Guide for FREE!!!

-- Subject: Do You Feel Hugged Yet?

-- Subject: Snuggle Up While You Can

Insurance Company

About Us

 The Anderson Insurance Company sells insurance. Whether you need life insurance or house insurance or health insurance, they sell it. They sell car insurance, too!

 The Anderson Insurance Company doesn't just sell insurance policies, it provides peace of mind. Whether it's life insurance, health insurance or insurance for your home or auto, we work with you to provide policies that cover your needs, whenever or wherever those needs may arise.

Press Release

 The Anderson Insurance Company is announcing they will be at the Main Street Health Fair giving out free insurance consultations. You must go!!! You won't want to miss it!

Anyone who wants to add a layer of security to their life can benefit from free insurance consultations from the Anderson Insurance Company at the Main Street Health Fair. Stop by the Anderson Insurance Company fair booth from 10 a.m. to 2 p.m. during the Oct. 19 fair for suggestions on health insurance and other types of policies that can meet your various needs.

News Article

Last Saturday on October 19 at 10 a.m., an informative time was had by all when the Anderson Insurance Company had a booth at the Main Street Health Fair and gave out free consultations. One agent said people learned a lot. "People learned a lot," he said.

Most attend the annual Main Street Health Fair for health-related reasons, and this year that health extended to homes and cars. Thanks to the free consultations offered by the Anderson Insurance Company at the fair, more than 200 folks received no-cost insurance guidance and more than 35 walked away with new policies for their home and vehicles.

Article

 The Anderson Insurance Company starts with "A," so they are at the top of the list alphabetically. Last month, they were at the top of the BBB list, too, when they received a special award. It was just one of many awards over the years and years of good, "A" service.

 A company name that starts with "A" isn't the only reason the Anderson Insurance Company is consistently at the top of the list of insurance providers. Its service has long merited top honors, including the recent Best National Insurance Provider award from the Better Business Bureau.

Blog Post

 You need home insurance to protect your home from fire and floods and other disasters. In fact, if you have a mortgage, the mortgage says you have to have home insurance so you can't get around it.

 Even if the law didn't require mortgaged homes to have home insurance, a house without it is a disaster waiting to happen. A careless candle, damaged pipe or all-out lashing by Mother Nature can-not only destroy your home but, without insurance, could destroy your life savings right along with it.

E-book

This e-book is going to explain how to figure out how to get the insurance policies you need to suit your very own needs. You will first look at things you need to protect and then you will see if you are protecting them the right way.

Yes, we know. Insurance is not the most exciting of topics, but it certainly ranks as one of the most important ones. We make it easy to ensure you have the coverage you need by offering a step-by-step analysis on your life's most important assets and revealing the types of coverage that can help keep them most secure.

BIO

John Anderson, founder of the Anderson Insurance Company, wrote a lot of books about insurance and finances and started his own insurance company named after him.

After a car crash left his family destitute due to inadequate insurance, John Anderson vowed to help others avoid a similar fate. He kicked off his mission by founding the Anderson Insurance Company and continues to educate consumers on the importance of proper coverage through his series of books that explore insurance and financial topics.

Review

The Anderson Insurance Company is really good because they really care. They aren't just out to make a quick buck even though they sold me all kinds of insurance.

Who knew I could get pet insurance for my dog? The Anderson Insurance Company did, thanks to its extensive industry knowledge and even deeper understanding of the types of insurance that would meet my unique needs.

Facebook

 Click here to see three types of insurance you might not even know existed. They are pet insurance, insurance for your shoes and another one that will make you surprised!

 Insurance for your shoe collection, your nose or your pet rabbit? You bet! Check out this trio of lesser-known insurance types that may actually come in handy.

(Tip: Take advantage of Facebook's ability to add photos.)

Twitter

 Weird and freaky insurance LOOK NOW!!!

 No, it's not weird to insure your shoes, your nose or your bunny rabbit. Check out 3 lesser-known insurance types.

RESOURCES: GUIDES AND DOWNLOADS

Byron White here, founder of WriterAccess. Hope this guide was as informative as it was enjoyable, as all good writing should be! By now you can see exactly what "more" you get when you pay more. As always, feedback is welcome to turn the good into the great.

(ByronWhite@WriterAccess.com)

Enjoy these resources that should help you win the war of words on the web.

Snap, Crackle and Pop Guide

WriterAccess.com/SnapCracklePop

Download a special guide called Snap, Crackle and Pop Your Content so it engages and converts. You can also view the recording of the presentation on this page.

Creative Brief Wizard

CreativeBriefWizard.com

Writers need a lot of information to create quality content. That's why we launched CreativeBriefWizard, a free tool for anyone to use that is pure white label—meaning there is not promotion for WriterAccess on the site.

The Content Marketing Roadmap

WriterAccess.com/ContentMarketingRoadmap

Download a PDF version of my first book *The Content Marketing Roadmap, Tips, Tools and Tactics to Win the War of Words on the Web.*

Content Marketing Webinars

WriterAccess.com/Webinar-Archive

Access live recordings of monthly content marketing webinars featuring host Byron White (that's me) and guest speakers—all leaders in the content marketing movement.

Speaking Events

WriterAccess.com/Speaking

I enjoy speaking on the content marketing topic at trade shows, webinars and corporate events. Matter of fact, I enjoy it so much, I don't charge any fees for the opportunity to help people learn about the topic and join the revolution.

RESOURCES: HOTSPOTS WORTH VISITING

Professional Associations

Editorial Freelancers Association

Rub elbows with writing pros from around the world, which means automatic contacts the next time you're in Indonesia.

the-efa.org

Association of Writers & Writing Programs

Like awards? So do they. Check out their perky lineup of contests along with grant and publishing opportunities.

awpwriter.org

American Amateur Press Association

The printed page is not dead! Just ask the AAPA folks. Supporters of printed press and journalism jazz since 1936.

aapainfo.org

International Center for Journalists

A must if you like digging deep into that political scandal or reporting that holds others accountable. Go get 'em, tiger!

icfj.org

The Authors Guild

Your backbone for protection, support and annoying legal things like copyright issues.

authorsguild.org

American Society of Journalists and Authors

True crime? Trade books? Magazine articles? Nonfiction reigns supreme with these precise and talented writers.

asja.org

Poets & Writers

Roses are red, violets are blue, if you write better poetry than this, this group is for you.

pw.org

American Copy Editors Society

They are NOT a bunch of "grammar geeks." They promise. But they'll still help save the world from dangling participles.

copydesk.org

National Novel Writing Month

Sign up to get tools and support to help you write that novel in a single month. For real!

nanowrimo.org

Small Publishers Artists and Writers Network

Sweet and sassy publishing-happy hub, come hither with questions, for market updates, publishing hints and tips.

spawn.org

Writers Guild of America East

More protection and support, this time on the East Coast.

wgaeast.org

Science Fiction and Fantasy Writers of America

Yes, Isaac Asimov was a member. No further promo required.

sfwa.org

The National Writers Union

Billed as the one and only labor union that represents freelance writers, complete with support from the UAW.

nwu.org

Writers Guild of America West

Writers for TV, movies, news, animation and new media can join up for instant connections and support.

wga.org

Society of Professional Journalists

Top newspaper folks are usually members of this one. Honorable mission is to keep the public in the know.

spj.org

The Professional Writers' Alliance

This group was created for "writers who sell" (not those who shove their work beneath the bed). And they'll even help you sell it!

professionalwritersalliance.groupsite.com

Publishing

AgentQuery

Got a book that needs a publisher? AgentQuery's at your service (in three easy steps!).

agentquery.com

Smashwords

Smashwords is a smash for self-published book distribution and exposure. Not to mention its super-cool name.

smashwords.com

Vook

Does doing e-book and print layout make you cringe? Let Vook do the painful stuff (then publish your book on demand).

vook.com

Duotrope

Hot-off-the-press listings that help you select and submit to the perfect publisher.

duotrope.com

BookRix

E-book distribution center that serves up a big chunk of profits (to you, not themselves).

bookrix.com

Hyperinks

Quick, amusing reads for super-busy people. Try it in the grocery store line!

hyperink.com

Technical Skills

OWL Exercise Pages

Keep your writing skills sharp as a stiletto with a keen cache of English exercises.

owl.english.purdue.edu/exercises/

Common Errors in English Usage

Helpful usage hints so you'll stop confusing "all right" with "alright" already.

public.wsu.edu/~brians/errors/errors.html

Guide to Grammar and Style

Make revisions a thing of the past by beefing up your grammar and style.

andromeda.rutgers.edu/~jlynch/Writing/a.html

Daily Grammar Lessons

A regular serving of grammatical lessons to wow the crowd at cocktail parties!

dailygrammarlessons.blogspot.com/

Community

The Writer

Sweet magazine, helpful articles, loads of resources and a slew of contests. Get going!

writermag.com

Writer Unboxed

Fabulous forum started by two aspiring novelists who needed a place to speak their minds.

writerunboxed.com

The Renegade Writer

Feisty, fast-paced blog posts with helpful tips, like how to deal with people who hate your writing (blffft!).

therenegadewriter.com

Writer's Digest

Long-published, writer-friendly mag packed with hints, tips, contests and opportunities.

writersdigest.com

Writer Beware

No-nonsense advice with "a special focus on the weird and wacky things" that go down on the fringes of the publishing world. Sold!

accrispin.blogspot.com

Absolute Write

Hopping blog with mounds of tips, resource links and an equally hopping forum.

absolutewrite.com

Scribophile

Massively active writing group for feedback, support and guidance. Maybe even friendships.

scribophile.com

Writing.com

All-levels forum kicking around since 2000. That's plenty of time to establish a friendly and creative environment. Go!

writing.com

FanStory

Feedback, contests and community provide a dazzling way to play with your writing.

fanstory.com

WritingForums

One humongous, massive, enormous, colossal, intriguing writers forum. Yeah, it's pretty impressive.

writingforums.org

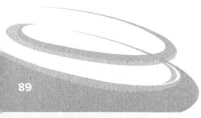

Writing Resources

WriterAccess Language Analysis

Find out if your writing is easy and breezy to read with this spot-on "readability" test.

writeraccess.com/language-analysis

ideaLaunch SEO Tools

Instant review of any web page to check if your SEO is stellar or stinks.

idealaunch.com/free-seo-tools/

WritersWeekly

A high-powered ezine to power up your freelance career.

writersweekly.com

OneLook

Fun with words gets a whole new meaning with this multi-functional online dictionary.

onelook.com

AP Stylebook

The journalism copy editors' "Bible." Bookmark it NOW.

apstylebook.com

All Indie Writers

Forget feel-good BS; this site cuts to the chase on how to thrive as a well-paid writer.

allfreelancewriting.com

Copyblogger

Groovy tips and tricks for creating and succeeding with your online content marketing.

copyblogger.com

The Chicago Manual of Style

The copyeditors' "Bible" for scientific writing and historical journals. Bookmark it if you write that stuff.

chicagomanualofstyle.org

Inkwell Editorial

Hilarious insights from a longtime and prolific freelancer. We betcha like her.

inkwelleditorial.com

Bartelby - The Elements of Style

Online version of that dusty old book we were forced to buy for English 101. Oh, the things we forget!

bartelby.com/141/

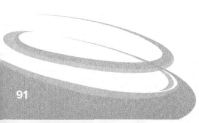

Copyscape

Plagiarism checking kingdom; make sure your work is 100% original – and no one's stealing your intellectual property.

copyscape.com

Grammarly

Like a grammar-czar correcting errors over your shoulder (but not as intimidating!).

grammarly.com

PlagiarismDetect.com

Another plagiarism checking kingdom if you tire of the same ole Copyscape. This one can also check in Spanish.

plagiarismdetect.com

ArticleChecker.com

Yet another kingdom for the plagiarism check. Get the hint yet? Check for plagiarism!

articlechecker.com

PaperRater

Free writing tool checks grammar, spelling and gives your work a quick once-over. Oh, yeah. It can also check for (drum roll please) plagiarism.

paperrater.com

AutoCrit

Get an instant editing overview of your manuscript without begging your mother and friends to read the thing.

autocrit.com

Ginger Software

Neat-o digital "personal assistant" checks your grammar, rephrases your sentences and even reads your text out loud.

gingersoftware.com

Jobs & Gigs

WriterAccess

Awesome online marketplace with a special touch for matching clients and writers to empower both. Full disclosure, that's us!

writeraccess.com

Freelance Writing

Articles, tutorials, contests, news, forums and gobs of other good-ies to help boost your career.

freelancewriting.com

Creative Hotlist

If you're writing is hot (and whose isn't?) head over to search for gigs and showcase your talents.

creativehotlist.com

Elance

Bid on jobs, find clients and connections, thrive in your writing and editing career.

elance.com

Mediabistro

One-stop job board for media work, complete with links to media-happy topics.

mediabistro.com

oDesk

Flourishing freelance job site for everyone from writers to sales folks with IT geniuses in between.

odesk.com

JournalismJobs.com

Go-to site if you're looking for newspaper, magazine or other journalism work.

journalismjobs.com

Freelance Writing Jobs | freelancewritinggigs.com

Career-boosting site stocked with job leads, writing tips and business help.

freelancewritinggigs.com

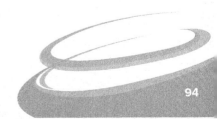

Guru.com

Create a profile and nab freelance jobs from clients around the world. (Their stats keep mentioning the word "millions.")

guru.com

Indeed

Time-saving, consolidated search that checks for gigs across job sites, newspapers, associations and company career pages.

indeed.com

FundsforWriters

Yes, you read that right. Money, money, money from grants, contests and high-end jobs.

fundsforwriters.com

Freelanced

Like Facebook for freelancers. But with jobs in the mix.

freelanced.com

Careerjet

Another time-saving search engine that scours through more than 27,000 websites for jobs of your choice.

careerjet.com

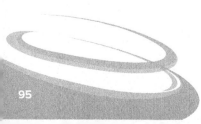

PeoplePerHour

Post the job you want to do, how much you want to get paid and then gear up for someone to bite.

peopleperhour.com

iFreelance

Job-posting site that connect clients directly with writers, kicking the middleman to the curb.

ifreelance.com

GateHouse Media

Go local and work close to home with the litany of listings for community publications and businesses.

gatehousemedia.com

Textbroker

Connect with gads of clients who need gads of writing jobs.

textbroker.com

Zerys

More than 30,000 writing jobs come down the pike every month at this place. Nab one!

zerys.com

Skyword

Platform that connects freelancers with top brands and companies. Sign in, create profile, get writing.

skyword.com

Contently

Set up an amazing near-instant profile that showcases loads of clips, complete with their overall word count (whew!)

contently.com

Demand Media

Videos, how-tos, features, informative articles, slideshows and more are what you can create if you hook up with this site.

demandmedia.com

CPSIA information can be obtained
at www.ICGtesting.com
Printed in the USA
LVOW01s1412210816

500870LV00001B/1/P